No Lex 10-12

J 921
RICE, JERRY

Jerry Rice

by Mark Stewart

ACKNOWLEDGMENTS

The editors wish to thank Jerry Rice for his cooperation in preparing this book.
Thanks also to Integrated Sports International for their assistance.

PHOTO CREDITS

All photos courtesy AP/Wide World Photos, Inc. except the following:

Rob Tringali, Jr./Sports Chrome – Cover, 13, 37 bottom right
San Francisco 49ers – 5 center right, 27, 32, 43
Rich Kane/Sports Chrome – 9, 46 top left
Louis Raynor/Sports Chrome – 19, 46 bottom right
Mark Stewart – 48

STAFF

Project Coordinator: John Sammis, Cronopio Publishing
Series Design Concept: The Sloan Group
Design and Electronic Page Makeup: Jaffe Enterprises, and
        Digital Communications Services, Inc.

LIBRARY OF CONGRESS CATALOGING-IN-PUBLICATION DATA

Stewart, Mark.
    Jerry Rice / by Mark Stewart.
        p. cm. – (Grolier all-pro biographies)
    Includes index.
    Summary: Profiles the record-beraking receiver, from his childhood in Mississippi to
his success with the San Francisco 49ers.
    ISBN 0-516-20171-9 (lib. binding) – 0-516-26019-7 (pbk.)
    Rice, Jerry–Juvenile literature. 2. Football players–United States–Biography–Juvenile
literature. 3. San Francisco 49ers (Football team)–Juvenile literature. [1. Rice, Jerry.
2. Football players. 3. Afro-Americans–Biography.]
I. Title. II. Series.
GV939.R53S84 1996
796.332'092–dc20
(B)   96-18381
                                                                                  CIP
                                                                                   AC

Grolier **ALL-PRO** Biographies™

Jerry Rice

by
Mark Stewart

CHILDREN'S PRESS®
A Division of Grolier Publishing
New York • London • Hong Kong • Sydney
Danbury, Connecticut

Contents

Who

Am I?

They say you can judge people by the company they keep. That may be so. But is it fair to evaluate an athlete based on who he is playing against? I broke a lot of records in high school and college, but because I was not playing against big-time teams, some people thought my accomplishments were not real. I learned that if you're really good at something, you will eventually find your way to the top. My name is Jerry Rice, and this is my story . . . "

"I learned that if you're really good at something, you will eventually find your way to the top."

Growing Up

Imagine a town so small that there are no stoplights, no sidewalks, and no street signs. Imagine a place where everyone not only knows one another, but they are all distantly related. This is what Crawford, Mississippi, was like when Jerry Rice was born in 1962. Less than 500 people lived in Crawford, and the next town was more than 25 miles away.

Jerry and his seven brothers and sisters lived in a house that his father had built. Joe Rice was a highly skilled mason. When Jerry was old enough, he asked if he could be his assistant during school holidays and summer breaks. That was fine, his father told him, but it would mean waking up at five in the morning and working hard all day in the hot sun. Jerry joined his older brothers in working with their father. The boys would mix cement and move bricks and lumber around the job site. When their father progressed to the second story of a construction project, the Rice boys would have to move bricks from the ground and make a new pile higher up. This was Jerry's specialty. He would stand atop the scaffolding and catch bricks that his brothers threw to him. Jerry started by catching two at a time, then three, and then four bricks at the same time! He concentrated so hard that the bricks seemed to be going in slow motion. This skill made Jerry his father's favorite assistant, and it would really pay off when he became a football receiver.

Jerry liked growing up in Crawford. There always seemed to be a game of some sort going on, and he was always invited to play. Jerry loved running, jumping, catching, and just being outside. It never got very cold where he lived, so he could play outdoor sports all year long. He also loved to read about sports. "I used to read *Sports Illustrated* and other magazines in the library all the time," Jerry remembers.

Jerry never seems to grow old. He's in as good shape today as when he was growing up.

To this day, Jerry recognizes the importance of reading. "Everything you do revolves around reading. I wasn't thinking about being a professional athlete when I was a kid, and I am very glad that I developed good reading skills when I did. It definitely comes in handy. If you think you can become a football player without being able to read well, you'd better think again—one of the most difficult things you'll ever have to read is an NFL playbook!"

As Jerry grew older, he began to wonder about the world outside of Crawford. He and his friends often talked about what it would take to get out of rural Mississippi, but Jerry was one of the few who did something about it. He worked extra hard at everything, from sports to schoolwork. Jerry was one of the top students at his elementary school. He liked all of his classes, but sometimes he grew distracted when it came time to do his homework. Jerry preferred to play football or ride the horses in his neighbor's field, but his parents would have none of that. They made sure that his assignments were done before he went to bed, and they told him that the only way he would be allowed to play sports was if he continued to do well in school.

Jerry went to high school at B. L. Moor, which served several of the communities in Mississippi's Oktibbeha County—

one of the poorest counties in the United States. Many of the classes were held in temporary trailers, but that did not bother Jerry. He was there to learn. He knew his best chance to be successful was to get into college, and that meant his grades and test scores would have to be excellent.

Still, temptation sometimes got the best of Jerry, and one day early in his sophomore year, he was caught cutting class by the school principal, Ezell Wicks. Jerry was so scared he just turned and ran. Mr. Wicks knew who he was—there were less than two dozen students in Jerry's class—and the next day he called the young man into his office to be disciplined. Part of Jerry's punishment was that he had to report to the football coach. Mr. Wicks may have been angry, but he was not stupid. Anyone who could move as fast as Jerry had the day before belonged on the football team!

Although Jerry's older brother, Tom, had been a good player for Moor, Jerry never really thought about playing high-school football until he met with Coach Charlie Davis that day. While playing catch, they discussed the idea of his trying out for the team. Jerry decided he would do it, then he went home to tell his parents. His mother was against it. She thought he was too skinny. But the more she protested, the more determined Jerry became. Finally, she gave up and let him play.

Jerry developed into a terrific receiver and won All-Conference honors that year. He was the team's best player and hardest worker. He never seemed to get tired, and it never bothered him that the school could not afford good equipment or a decent playing field. In his last two seasons, Jerry led the team to 18 wins and only 2 losses. In his senior year, he caught 88 passes in 10 games and earned All-Conference honors for the third straight time.

Jerry knew that football was his ticket to an education. Tom had been offered a scholarship by Jackson State University and had achieved tremendous success both in the classroom and on the field. During Jerry's senior year, he kept looking in the stands to see if he could spot college scouts. He never did see any, because they never came. And when it was time to consider scholarship offers, not a single Division I school wanted him. Jerry was particularly disappointed that Mississippi State University showed no interest. Between his good grades and his football skills, he believed he should have been at the top of the school's recruiting list.

In the end, he took Tom's advice and accepted a scholarship from Mississippi Valley State University. It was a small Division I-AA school, but Jerry's brother told him that it had the kind of passing offense that would enable him to stand out. Jerry graduated from B. L. Moor as a member of the Class of 1980. Their motto was: *If there is no struggle, there is no progress.* As Jerry packed his bags for college, he turned these words over in his mind.

Jerry was drafted from one of the least-known colleges by the high-profile San Francisco 49ers.

College

The difference between attending a big Division I school and a tiny Division I-AA college was apparent to Jerry Rice from the first day he joined the Mississippi Valley State football team. Each player was handed one Delta Devils uniform and told that they had to make it last all season long. It was to be washed and dried after each practice—by the players themselves! The team's coach was Archie Cooley. His nickname was "Gunslinger," because he loved to let his quarterback fire away. Coach Cooley told Jerry that he was to be the offense's primary receiver and predicted that he would be unstoppable. By Jerry's sophomore year, Cooley's prediction came true. That season, he and freshman quarterback Willie Totten hooked up for 66 completions and more than 1,000 yards.

In 1983, Jerry caught 102 passes and scored 14 touch-

Years

downs. He was only a junior, but already he was being called the finest pro prospect in the Southwest Athletic Conference. His teammates called him "World," because there was nothing in the world he could not catch. And no one in the world could catch Jerry once he had the ball, especially during his senior year, when he scored 28 touchdowns.

In 1984, the Delta Devils completed the regular season with a 9–1 record and averaged more than 60 points a game. Jerry caught more passes and gained more yards than any receiver in the country, and he shattered 18 Division I-AA records. Unfortunately, he remained a virtual unknown to most college football fans. MVSU was such a small school that it received little national attention. Jerry knew he was not getting enough publicity when he met a young woman named

Jackie Mitchell while attending a basketball game. She was a student at nearby Southern Mississippi, yet she had never heard of Jerry! He asked if he could call her, and she gave him her phone number. Jerry and Jackie soon began dating, and they eventually got married.

During his senior year in college, Jerry knew he was good enough to have a pro career. But did the pros know it? Most did not. Because Jerry had amassed his amazing numbers against "second-rate" players, many NFL teams ignored him completely. Those who did scout him were unimpressed by his speed in the 40-yard dash. What they did not understand is that Jerry is one of those rare athletes who is actually faster chasing down a pass in a helmet and pads than he is wearing a T-shirt and a pair of shorts!

Jerry's stats at Mississippi Valley State University:

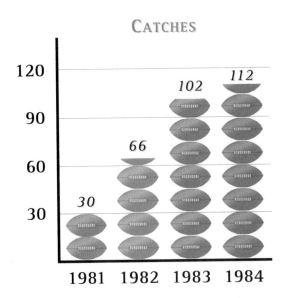

CATCHES

30 — 1981
66 — 1982
102 — 1983
112 — 1984

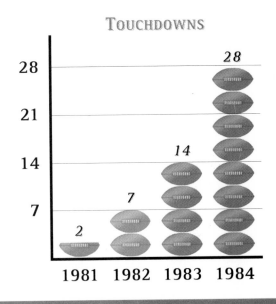

TOUCHDOWNS

2 — 1981
7 — 1982
14 — 1983
28 — 1984

Road to the

The key moment in the 1985 NFL draft actually took place several months earlier, on a Saturday evening in October 1984. San Francisco 49ers head coach Bill Walsh decided to take a break from preparing for the next day's game against the Houston Oilers. He turned on the television just in time to see a clip of Jerry Rice scoring a touchdown for an obscure college in Mississippi. "Nice catch," Walsh thought. Then he saw highlights of Jerry scoring four more touchdowns. "Who is this guy?" Walsh wondered. He knew then that if the 49ers did not grab Jerry in the draft, they would have to play against him one day. And that was not something Walsh looked forward to.

On draft day, the 49ers had the 28th pick in the first round. Fearing that the receiver-hungry Dallas Cowboys might take Jerry with the number-17 pick, San Francisco made a trade with the New England Patriots to move up to the 16th position. They were not sure if the Cowboys had "discovered"

Super Bowl

Jerry, but they were unwilling to take the chance. Meanwhile, everyone was dying to know who the 49ers wanted so badly. When they announced Jerry's name, no one could believe

that Walsh would waste a first-round pick on someone from a nothing little school. Walsh just smiled. He knew he had just picked the best player in the draft.

Jerry's rookie season did not start well, as he dropped 11 passes in his first 11 games. He also heard the unfamiliar sound of booing from the fans at San Francisco's Candlestick Park. "I had never been booed

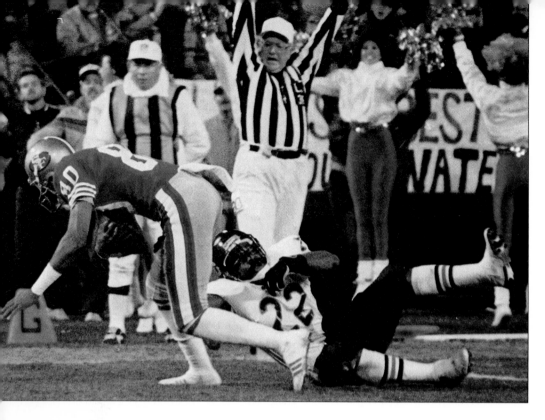

Jerry takes a short pass in the end zone to tie an NFL record for touchdowns in 11 consecutive games.

in my life," Jerry says. "I felt like taking off my uniform and just going to the locker room." Finally, in a Monday night game against the Los Angeles Rams, Jerry had the first great game of his pro career. He caught 10 passes for 241 yards. Jerry finished the season with 49 catches for 927 yards and was named NFC Rookie of the Year.

In 1986, Jerry began using special receiver's gloves. He also became more comfortable with San Francisco's complex offensive strategy. The result was a league-leading 1,570 receiving yards, which at the time was third-best total in

NFL history. In 1987, Jerry established a new NFL mark with 22 touchdown catches despite playing in just 12 games. Imagine what his numbers would have been had he played the usual 16 games! He led the NFL with 138 points scored and received the Player of the Year award. All that remained was a Super Bowl ring.

Jerry hobbled through the 1988 season with a sore ankle, yet still managed to have a nice year. The 49ers struggled, too, needing four victories in their last five games to win the division title. But Jerry and his teammates regained their killer instinct once the Super Bowl was within striking distance. He caught two touchdowns in each of the team's two playoff games, then dazzled a national audience with his performance in the Super Bowl. Jerry made one clutch reception after

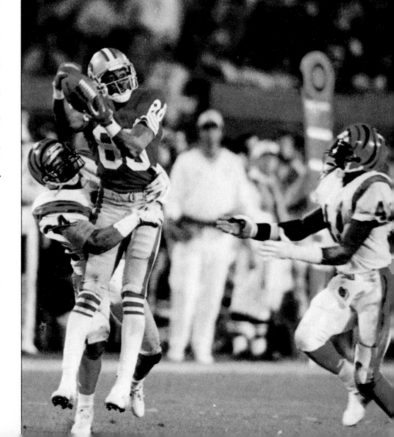

Jerry hauls in a touchdown pass during the 1989 Super Bowl.

Jerry breaks the single-season receiving record during a 1995 game against the Atlanta Falcons.

another in a dramatic come-from-behind victory over the Cincinnati Bengals. The 49ers were NFL champions. And Jerry was named the game's MVP.

Since then, Jerry has earned two more Super Bowl rings and another Player of the Year trophy. He has also caught more passes for more yards and more touchdowns than anyone in NFL history. In 1995, he shattered the single-season mark for receiving yards, when he finished with 1,848. Although he still has many more great seasons ahead of him, Jerry has already established himself as the finest receiver in the history of professional football.

Jerry Rice has caught more passes than any receiver in NFL history.

Timeline

1987: Sets NFL record with 22 touchdown catches

1985: Named NFC Rookie of the Year

1989: Named MVP of Super Bowl XXIII

1995: Ties his own Super Bowl record with three touchdowns against the San Diego Chargers

1994: Leads the NFL in receiving yards for the fifth time in his career

1996: Named MVP of the 1996 Pro Bowl

Game

Jerry holds up the football after setting an all-time NFL receiving record in 1995.

In 1984, Jerry finished ninth in the voting for the Heisman Trophy, despite attending little-known Mississippi Valley State University.

Jerry led the NFL in receiving yards for the sixth time in 1995. His 1,848 yards set an all-time record. "As a competitor, I always want the football. I'm not selfish, I just want the opportunity to prove to myself that I can do it."

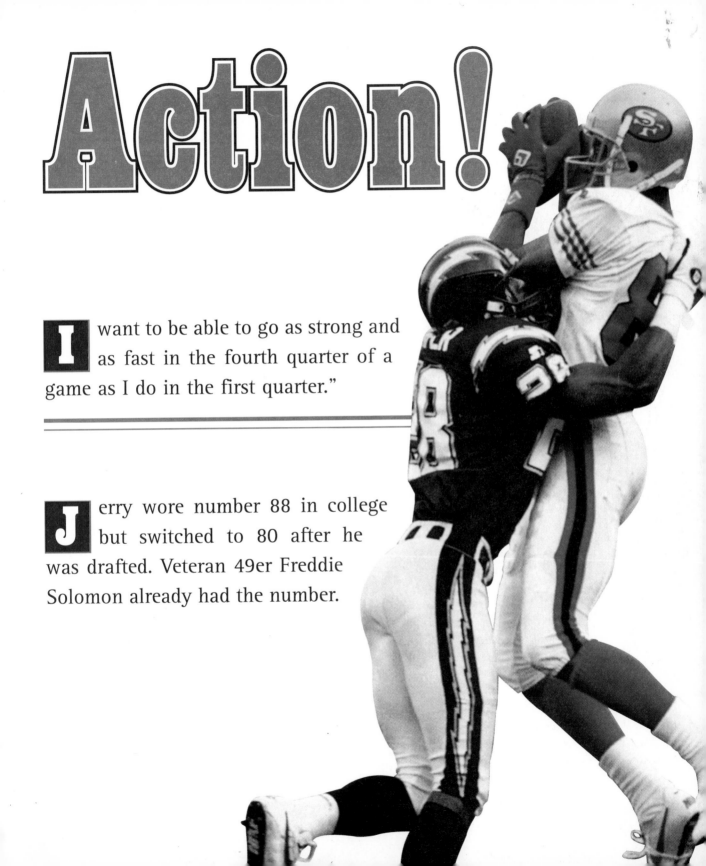

Action!

I want to be able to go as strong and as fast in the fourth quarter of a game as I do in the first quarter."

J erry wore number 88 in college but switched to 80 after he was drafted. Veteran 49er Freddie Solomon already had the number.

Part of Jerry's success is due to his quarterbacks. For years, Jerry caught passes from Joe Montana. "I admire Joe Montana for the way he handled himself in pressure situations. He was truly one of the greatest quarterbacks ever to play the game."

On October 14, 1990, Jerry equaled an NFL record with five touchdown catches against the Atlanta Falcons.

San Francisco quarterback Steve Young (#8)

When Steve Young became the 49er quarterback, Jerry had to adjust to his throws. Because Young is a lefty, his ball spins differently and tails off in a different direction than Jerry was used to.

Jerry uses his hands to get away from Dallas Cowboys defender Deion Sanders.

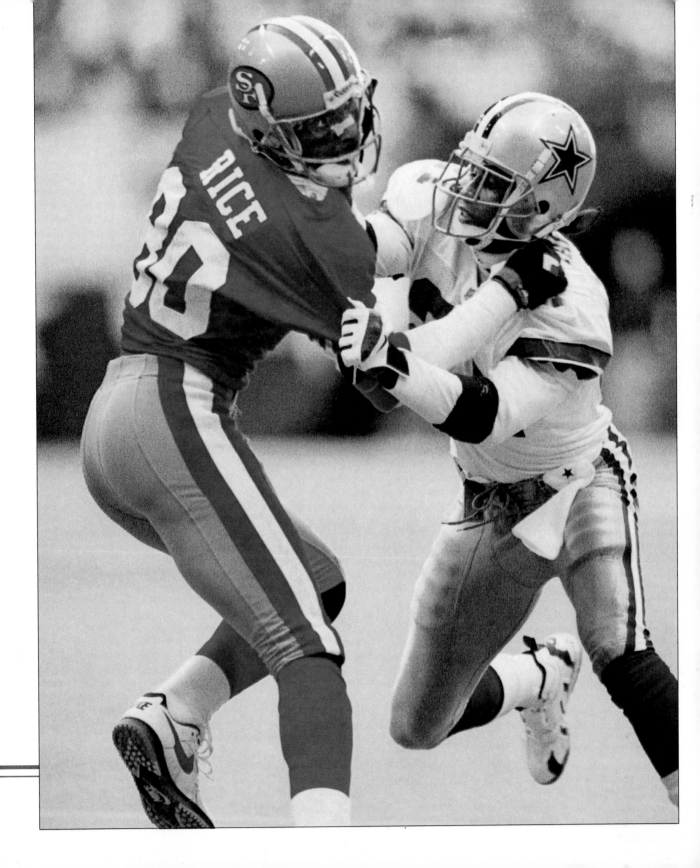

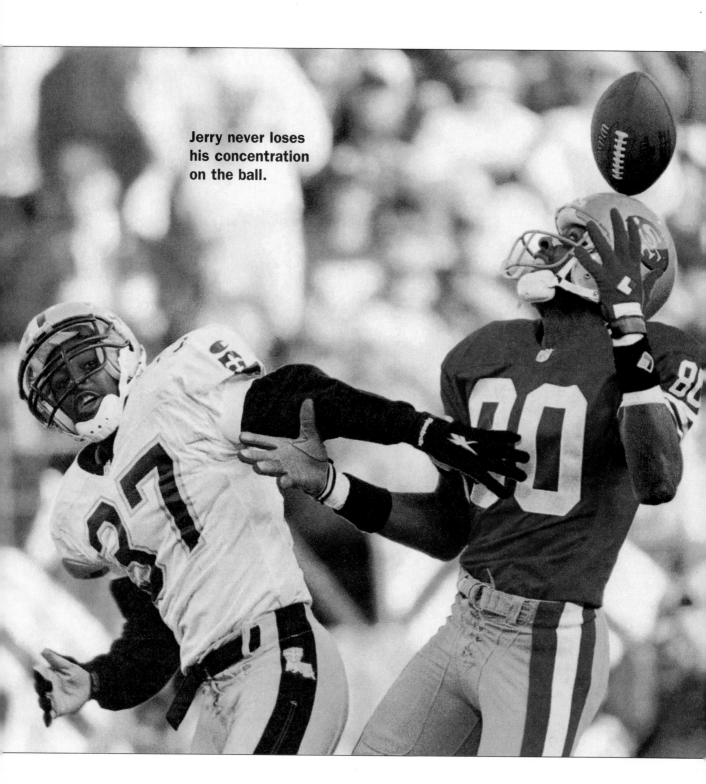

Jerry never loses
his concentration
on the ball.

In such a glorious career, what is Jerry's favorite moment? "It is hard to pick out my proudest moment, but the touchdown I scored against the Raiders in 1994 to set the all-time mark was very special. It was my 127th career touchdown and set an NFL record."

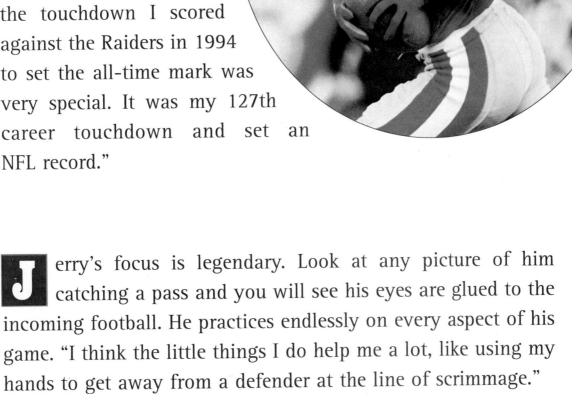

Jerry's focus is legendary. Look at any picture of him catching a pass and you will see his eyes are glued to the incoming football. He practices endlessly on every aspect of his game. "I think the little things I do help me a lot, like using my hands to get away from a defender at the line of scrimmage."

HOW DOES

According to Jerry Rice, the thing that makes a good receiver great is the ability to speed up, or accelerate, while making a move. Speed is useless if you have to slow down to make a sharp cut. But if you can speed up while cutting, then you stand a good chance of losing your man and breaking into the open.

"I accelerate into my cuts. Sprinters don't do that—they don't have the body control you need. They chop their steps going into cuts. I accelerate into my cuts, and accelerate again out of them. That way I'm on top of a defender immediately and then I'm past him. Sometimes, I even amaze myself."

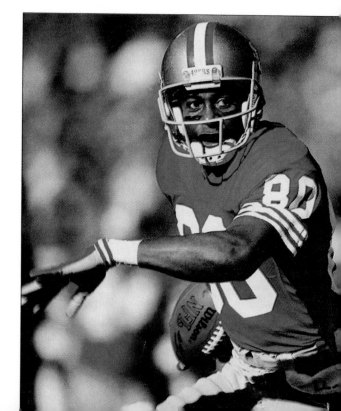

He Do It?

The Grind

When you are the NFL's all-time leading receiver—and have one of the most recognizable faces in all of football—it is hard to leave your house without being mobbed by adoring fans. Jerry Rice knows that this is the price he must pay for being a celebrity, but he still considers it the toughest part of life as a professional athlete.

"The hardest thing is definitely the lack of privacy. You can't really go anywhere with your family because people always want to get an autograph or take a picture with you. I know it comes with the territory, but you can never get used to it."

Above: Jerry is interviewed by
ESPN broadcaster Sterling
Sharpe during a break at practice.

Below: Fans ask Jerry to sign almost
anything before the 1996 Pro Bowl.

Say What?

Here's what football people are saying about Jerry Rice:

"From the first moment I saw him, he was the best I ever saw."

—*Dwight Clark, former teammate*

"You expect Jerry Rice to make the catch. You never wonder what's going to happen, you just expect it. And that's the mark of a great player."

—*Lynn Swann, all-time great receiver*

"He's the fastest, toughest, quickest, and has the most stamina. He's the best receiver in football."

—*Ray Perkins, former Tampa Bay Buccaneers coach*

"He's poetry in motion. I love watching him on TV, but then I think, 'Oh no, I've got to cover him!'"

—*Mark Collins, Kansas City Chiefs cornerback*

"Rice is the complete wide receiver. He has the unique ability to be a game-breaker. He can catch possession passes consistently, and he's a great blocker for the running game."

—*Paul Warfield, Hall of Fame receiver*

"I think he believes that if they covered him with eleven guys, he should still get open and win the game."

—*Steve Young, 49ers teammate*

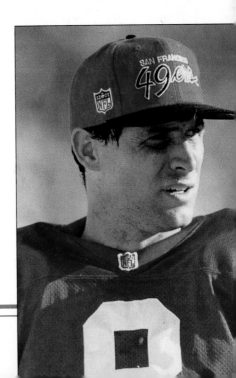

Career

For the rest of his career, Jerry Rice will enjoy a feeling few other athletes in history have experienced. Each time he catches a pass, gains a yard, or scores a touchdown, he will be adding to his own all-time NFL records. Yet unlike most career record-holders, Jerry is not fading at the end of his career. In 1995, he established a new mark for receiving yards in a season, and caught a personal-best 122 passes. Jerry's records may very well be broken one day, but he is not making it easy on the next guy!

Highlights

Despite playing for a Division I-AA school, Jerry was an All-America selection in his senior year. His 27 touchdown catches that season are the most ever by a college player.

No college player has ever caught more passes or amassed more receiving yards than Jerry.

On October 1, 1983, Jerry caught 24 passes against Southern University to establish a new NCAA record.

Jerry holds career Super Bowl records with 42 points, 7 touchdowns, 28 catches, and 512 receiving yards. He also established a new single-game standard for touchdowns when he scored three against the Broncos in Super Bowl XXIV. He equaled this mark in Super Bowl XXIX when he scored three times against the Chargers.

Jerry gets a hug from teammate Randy Cross after
he set a record with 19 touchdown catches in 1987.

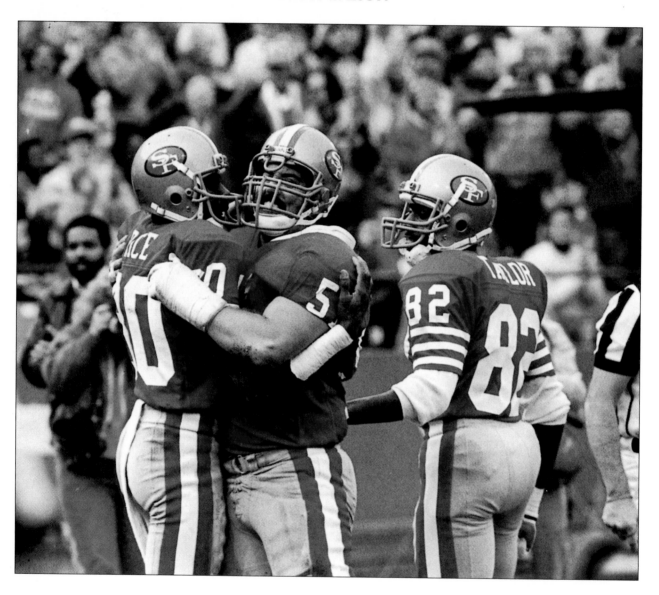

On December 27, 1987, Jerry caught a touchdown in his 13th consecutive game to establish an all-time record.

Jerry's 17 touchdowns, 1,656 receiving yards, and 111 catches in post-season play are NFL records.

Jerry's 154 touchdowns are the most in NFL history. His 22 touchdown catches in the strike-shortened 1987 season are the most ever by a receiver.

No player has ever had more 1,000-yard seasons than Jerry, who has topped that mark every year since 1986.

Jerry was named NFL Player of the Year in 1987 and 1990.

On December 18, 1995, Jerry established a new personal best with 289 yards against the Minnesota Vikings.

Jerry gets congratulations from his Pro Bowl teammates on his way to being named the 1996 MVP.

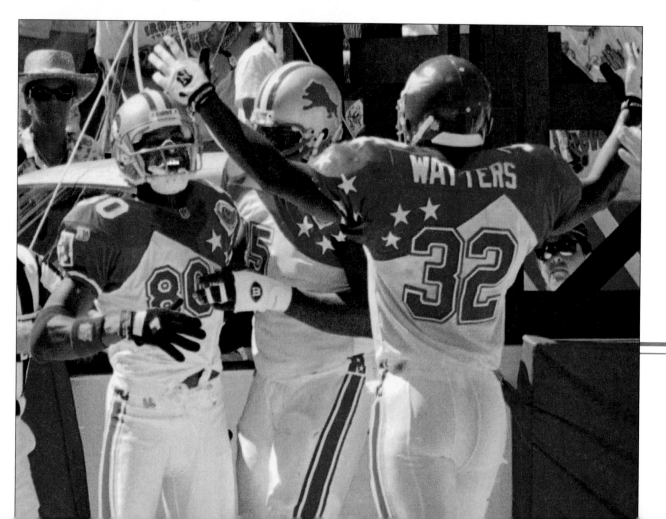

Jerry runs wild against the Minnesota Vikings.

Jerry has been named a Pro Bowl starter 10 years in a row.

Jerry has run the ball 69 times in his NFL career and scored touchdowns on nine of those runs!

Numbers

Name: Jerry Lee Rice

Nickname: "Flash"

Born: October 13, 1962

Height: 6' 2"

Weight: 200 pounds

Uniform Number: 80

College: Mississippi Valley State University

Jerry is the only player in history to have three 100-catch seasons in his career.

Year	Team	Games	Catches	Yards	Yards Per Catch	Touchdown Catches	Team Record
1985	San Francisco 49ers	16	49	927	18.9	3	10-6
1986	San Francisco 49ers	16	86	1,570*	18.3	15*	10-5-1
1987	San Francisco 49ers	12	65	1,078	16.6	22*	13-2
1988	San Francisco 49ers	16	64	1,306	20.4	9	10-6**
1989	San Francisco 49ers	16	82	1,483*	18.1	17*	14-2**
1990	San Francisco 49ers	16	100*	1,502*	15.0	13*	14-2
1991	San Francisco 49ers	16	80	1,206	15.1	14*	10-6
1992	San Francisco 49ers	16	84	1,201	14.3	10	14-2
1993	San Francisco 49ers	16	98	1,503*	15.3	15*	10-6
1994	San Francisco 49ers	16	112	1,499*	13.4	13	13-3**
1995	San Francisco 49ers	16	122	1,848*	15.1	15	11-5
Totals		172	944	15,123	16.0	146	129-45-1

*Led League
**Won Super Bowl

What If...

At my position, losing a step to age or injury can cost you your job. In that respect, I've been very fortunate to have played so many years, and by continuing to work hard I believe I will be able to play at this high level for many more. Had an injury forced me to quit pro football, I believe I would have tried my luck on the professional golf tour. Golf is a wonderful game that requires focus and discipline, and I'm sorry I didn't discover it sooner. Of course, with the education I received in college, I could have entered a number of other fields, too. My feeling is that no matter what you want to be—a football player, an attorney, a mechanic, whatever—the important thing is to just do it to the best of your ability, and be the very best you can be."

Glossary

COMPLEX difficult; hard to understand

CONDEMN to declare guilty of wrongdoing; to convict

CONSECUTIVE several events that follow one after another

AMASSED gathered; collected over time

APPARENT seemingly obvious; appearing as if to be clearly understood

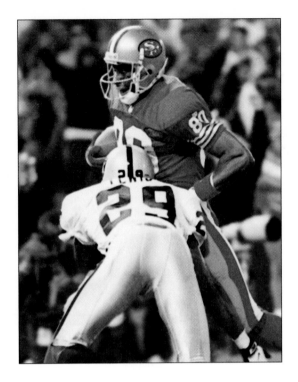

MASON one who builds a structure by laying stones or bricks

OBSCURE unknown; not prominent or famous

PROSPECT something that is looked forward to and expected

RECRUITING asking people to join a team or an organization

RURAL of or relating to country life

SCAFFOLD a movable platform for workers to stand or sit on when working high above the ground

SCHOLARSHIP money given to a student to help pay for schooling

STAMINA strength; endurance; staying power

UNIQUE singular; one of a kind

VETERAN one who has a lot of experience

Index

About The Author

Mark Stewart grew up in New York City in the 1960s and 1970s—when the Mets, Jets, and Knicks all had championship teams. As a child, Mark read everything about sports he could lay his hands on. Today, he is one of the busiest sportswriters around. Since 1990, he has written close to 500 sports stories for kids, including profiles on more than 200 athletes, past and present. A graduate of Duke University, Mark served as senior editor of *Racquet*, a national tennis magazine, and was managing editor of *Super News*, a sporting goods industry newspaper. He is the author of every Grolier All-Pro Biography.